Letters to

My Daughter

A collection of short stories and poems about
Love, Pride, & Identity

Nancy Arroyo Ruffin

Letters to My Daughter was nominated for Latino Literacy Now's 2014 International Latino Book Award for Best Poetry Book - English

La Grifa originally appeared in the book Welcome to Heartbreak

To the Beat of the Drum originally appeared in the on-line magazine La Respuesta, December 2013 Edition 6 Vol. 1

Third Printing, May 2014

Letters to My Daughter is published by
CreativeINK Publishing
Bergenfield, NJ 07621
nancyruffin@gmail.com

Cover Design and Concept by
Sal Acosta
s.artist22@yahoo.com
917.774.1320

ISBN: 0615789153

ISBN-13: 978-0615789156

DEDICATION

To my daughter Avarie Luz,
you have given me a new purpose in life.
Thank you for re-awakening my soul.

TABLE OF CONTENTS

Part III: For the Elders

ACKNOWLEDGMENTS

Thank you to all in my past, present, and future who have paved the way for me with their blood, sweat, commitment, and drive. To my parents, sister, family, friends, and those who came before me. Most importantly, to my husband and daughter whom without, my life would be meaningless.

PART I:

FOR THE BABIES

The baby who trails her scent like a flag of surrender through your life when there will be no more coming after - oh, that's love by a different name. She is the angel you hold in your arms for an hour after she's gone to sleep. If you put her down in the crib, she might wake up changed and fly away. So instead you rock by the window, drinking the light from her skin, breathing exhaled dreams. Your heart bays to the double crescent moon of closed lashes on her cheeks. She's the one you can't put down.

Barbara Kingsolver

A poem for Avarie

A lifetime half-lived

waiting to be blessed

with the valuable gift

of your precious life.

A dream finally realized

because some things

can't be rushed.

Knowing that in this time

and in this place

you were made for me.

I will cherish my new title

with gratitude.

Knowing that

I have finally been chosen

to experience

a love like no other.

That, which is shared

between a mother and child.

A mother's confession

There are days that I don't think about you at all.

You hide yourself well

often appearing when I least expect it.

I see you in her smiling eyes.

I hear you in her coos.

I feel you in her embrace.

I smell you in her scent, as I hold her tightly

while she tugs gently on my face

knowing that she is secure in my arms.

But she is only a child,

innocent to the devils that disguise themselves

as love,

protection,

safety.

Because even those who say they love you, hurt you.

Fear you consume me.

My life is no longer my own.

I belong to her and I am afraid

that I won't always be able

to protect her

to shield her

to guard her.

I try to let you go, but every day you return

and every day I welcome you back in.

What I always wanted

was to feel her touch like inspiration.

Bright eyes greet me hello every morning

the way the horizon welcomes the sun at dawn.

She is heaven

I want to live in her forever.

Teach her how beautiful she is

not because of how she looks

but because of who she is.

Teach her that she is noble.

Fill her up with love

so that she learns

from an early age

that she is worthy of

love,

respect,

admiration.

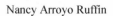

Babies are bits of star-dust blown from the hand of God. Lucky the woman who knows the pangs of birth for she has held a star.

Larry Barretto

Star Dust

TODAY IS HER BIRTHDAY. After 41 weeks of pregnancy Avarie Luz Ruffin entered the world on July 27, 2012 at 10:21 a.m. weighing 7lbs 10oz and measuring 20 inches long. It was a beautiful summer day complete with sunny blue skies and warm 87 degree temperature.

The delivery just like the weather was perfect. My private room at North Shore LIJ Medical Center was like a suite at a posh hotel. It was equipped with a private bathroom, a flat screen TV, a pull out sofa, had an amazing view, and was big enough to accommodate the dozen or so family members that came to visit. I didn't feel like I was at a hospital at all.

I imagine that's why the room was designed the way it was, to make the new moms feel as comfortable and as relaxed as possible. While my labor lasted only 5 hours there are many women who undergo hours sometimes even days bringing new life into this world. After enduring such an exhausting experience, it is nice to have a room like this to retreat to.

The contractions came unexpectedly yesterday during my non-stress test. As I sat in the cold reclining chair while the machine monitored the baby's heartbeat, I knew that I would not make it to my pre-natal appointment that was scheduled for today. Depending on the outcome of the appointment, the doctor was going to have me scheduled to be admitted so that she could induce my labor. I knew that wasn't going to be necessary. I knew that Avarie would come on her own, when she was ready, and she did.

Labor for me was not at all as I had imagined it to be. Maybe I prepared myself for the worst. I'd heard so many birth stories from family members and friends. Stories of the excruciating pain, of the countless hours spent pushing and breathing and cursing of spouses for putting us in this predicament and yet I don't remember experiencing any of that. There was some pain of course, but once I got the shot of epidural the pain subsided. I was admitted around 5 a.m. and by 10:21 a.m. I was holding her in my arms. For me, labor was a beautiful and peaceful experience. For that moment God made me his vessel. He used me to bring her into this world. He chose me. She chose me. To be the person entrusted with her life, her safety, her well-being.

"Birth is the sudden opening of a window, through which you look out upon a stupendous prospect. For what has happened? A miracle. You have exchanged nothing for the possibility of everything." William MacNeile Dixon

Her dad and I created a miracle. That is what she is. That is what we all are. We have to constantly remind ourselves that we are miracles. We are not here by mistake. Our lives have a purpose and we need to remember this whenever we feel down about ourselves. We must remember this when someone we love breaks our heart. When someone we trust, betrays us. When someone spreads a rumor that we know isn't true. We must remember this whenever we doubt ourselves and our magnificence. We are made in God's image and that alone makes us perfect.

Avarie is only a few hours old and I can't believe that I ever lived a life without her. My heart hurts from how much I love her. And not hurts in a bad way, but it is so full of love for her that it feels as if it is going to burst right through my chest. I never knew a love like this was possible and she will never know it either until she has a child of her own. I remember my mother saying that to me and now I completely understand what she meant.

The second I held Avarie in my arms I knew she was the reason for my existence. I was born to be her mother. When the doctor pulled her out of my body the joy on her father's face is unlike anything I have ever seen during the time we have been together. As I watched the tears fall from his eyes, I knew that from that moment our lives were forever changed. Her birth confirmed for me that every obstacle we encountered on this journey was worth it. She was meant to be our baby.

The chosen (part II)

There is an old Sufi myth that says

the child chooses the mother

before they are conceived.

They search and search

until they find the perfect place

to settle like Columbus did

in search for a new world.

Now here I am

a woman worthy

to hold the title of mother

for a child has finally chosen me

to be its home, life sentenced protector.

Created to breathe life into her lungs.

Birth seeds of hope from my ovaries

that will flourish into a future

writer, artist, or world leader.

Beauty that is wrapped

in golden sheets of new beginnings.

Carrying within it

my heart's deepest desire.

Magnificent one, all mine,

you are a colossal presence,

like a new moon in an empty sky

the tides of your love

a magnetic, gravitational pull.

You are

in the strength of my bones

in the curve of my muscles

in the crown of my hair

in the nape of my neck

in the gentleness of my hands

in the richness of my blood

in the light of my shadow.

No longer driven

by the restless urge to create

you are my masterpiece.

Like nights, spent under Parisian skies

viewing paintings at the Louvre.

Bathing in spiritual love,

I manifested you into existence.

My time has come

to hold you in my arms,

to love and nurture the soul

that has come to me in human form.

My womb no longer weeps.

The months, now reminders

that you are getting older,

getting stronger,

and will soon have dreams of your own.

I see you stare back at me

as I rock you to sleep at night.

A soul meant to be,

brown-eyed, laughing.

Above the air I breathe,

heavy rainclouds no longer shed tears.

Sadness has been replaced by your laugh.

Your eyes are the color of happiness.

My heart is now complete

because I have been chosen.

Asphalt dreams (on Palmetto Street)
(for Meryl and Vanessa)

A tree grew in Brooklyn

and so did my dreams

on the cracked asphalt

of tenement building stoops

a flower trying to break through

but roses don't bloom here

that's what I was told.

Never believing that I could ever see

a world beyond my periphery.

Struggling with tunnel vision

I watch passersby

and they watch me

holding my baby close.

Never expecting me

to flourish from

unfertilized potential.

For years,

I've sat here

playing hide and seek with the shade

afraid to feel the sun's gentle kiss,

knowing that its warmth is only temporary.

But I was raised a warrior.

Dodging verbal bullets of

"you will never amount to much"
because young mothers never do.
Words that bore blisters on my spirit.
The unbearable weight of shame
pierced through my skin like daggers.
Uncertainty became my daily make-up.
Dressed up in fear,
like I was wearing my Sunday best
I was broken.

Menacing memories leave me maimed
wanting to crawl back into uterine walls
before aspirations were deceased.
Somber portraits of deferred dreams
sing soliloquies into succulent black holes
of unfulfilled destinies.
But fate has not cheated me of everything
because here you are giving me
a second chance to sew back
the threads of life I severed
in order to survive.

In your eyes I see possibility
In your smile, security
Your embrace reminds me that
I am:
Strength

Courage

Survivor

Teacher

Creator

Woman

Mother

You are the hello that greets me

every morning like the rising sun.

With you I want to build legacies

Ancestral ties bind us to greatness

I must set expectations high

so that

You,

Me,

We,

Never settle for less.

For the daughters I didn't give birth to
(Marissa & Danielle)

Mommy you will never call me

for that title belongs to someone else.

Yet you will always be my child

for I have been there to see you grow

like the flowers of a royal water lily

and its many transformations.

Petals white as jades

full of virginal innocence

releasing aromatic scents of independence

that will attract many suitors

trying to strip you of your beauty

and rob you of your virtue.

So I say,

bask in the richness of your soul

for the light that you have within

can never be dimmed

unless you allow it.

Listen up young people…

Shattered dreams

always drown

in pools of potential

once full of promise.

Blood In Blood Out...

Chalk lines

    are all that remain

        as reminders of

            life taken too soon.

Dear Langston Hughes

This is for the kids who die
because kids will certainly die
in schools, in parks, on their way home, on their front stoops
while politicians lobby for stop and frisk,
violating rights of illegal search and seizure.

Kids will die in the morning,
in the afternoon, and in the evening after the nightly news.
No more Saturday morning cartoons
only Saturday mourning   vigils.

Families holding 9 day rosarios
Chanting:
Dios te salve Maria.
Llena eres de gracia.
El Señor es contigo.
Bendita tú eres
entre todas las mujeres.
Y bendito es el fruto de tu vientre Jesús.

This is for the kids who die
reciting scriptures,
memorizing psalms,
praying for salvation
from a God who will only love them

if they're holy,

and Christian,

and straight.

For the kids who believe

they are an abomination.

For the ones who are bullied

committing suicide

because only in death can they find peace.

This is for the kids who die

misinformed, misunderstood, mistreated, mistaken

for a gun toting thug

whose only crime

is the color of their skin.

Victims of neighborhood watches

but who watches that vigilante

who's stalking (I mean) watching you?

Of course,

the astute and the educated

who provide expert opinions

and the ones who are called sir and madam

white, black, brown, and yellow

who pen essays and write books

will live on creating words

to suffocate the memories

of the kids who die.

And the immoral lawyers,

and the corrupt cops,

and the fame hungry journalists,

and the wealth seeking ministers

will all turn their heads against the kids who die.
Turning a blind eye and whipping them
with silence, denials, and false testimonies
in order to fatten their pockets.

But listen kids who die,
someday your death will not be in vain.
One day they will build monuments
in your memory,
like Abraham Lincoln
or the honorable Dr. King.
And hands of all colors will unite,
voices will come together in laughter
and in joy and sing a song of honor
for all the kids who died.

Inspired by the poem For the Kids Who Die by Langston Hughes

There is a loneliness that can be rocked. Arms crossed, knees drawn up, holding, holding on, this motion, unlike a ship's, smooths and contains the rocker. It's an inside kind--wrapped tight like skin. Then there is the loneliness that roams. No rocking can hold it down. It is alive. On its own. A dry and spreading thing that makes the sound of one's own feet seem to come from a far-off place.

Toni Morrison, *Beloved*

The lost ones
(for the children of Sandy Hook)

Mothers sing hymns

of uncharted spaces

where earth meets sky,

and butterflies dance

against the tree lined milieu.

Shadows cower

beneath the shimmering

touch of the moon.

The morning paper

reports realities

of murdered children.

Police car sirens wail

street lights flicker

against concrete lawns.

Azure blue simplicities

before first impressions

were overlaid

by memories

of innocence

of loved ones

of lost ones

of high school graduations

that will never take place.

A letter to my daughter

July 27, 2013

It feels like I waited a lifetime for you and by other's standards I have. I was 35 when you were born. Most of my friends' children are already teenagers and here I am celebrating your first birthday. There are times when it all still seems so surreal to me. I feel like I am in the best dream that one day I am going to wake up from. This past year has been by far the very best year of my life. I love being a mother. I love being your mother.

You have filled a void in my heart that I didn't even realize was there until you were born. You have completed me. If I never do anything successful in my life it will not matter because you are the best thing I will ever create. My life has meaning now that you're here. My every thought is of you; of your well-being, and of your safety.

Sometimes I drive myself crazy thinking about the many ways I want to protect you. Almost to the point where I am afraid that I won't allow you to have normal childhood experiences because I'm frightened that you may get hurt.

I have never really been the type to worry much, but since you've been born I find that I worry all the time. I worry that you will stop breathing at night while you're sleeping. I worry that you'll develop some childhood disease that there's no cure for. I worry about you getting hurt or being mistreated. I watch stories on the news about children, who are kidnapped, abused, murdered and worry about what I can do to protect you from all of the evil that exists in this world.

It's a scary thing being a parent and from what I am told that fear never goes away. So here I am, a virtually new mother, trying to figure out how to love and protect you without isolating you or preventing you from growing up. I still don't know how to reconcile the two, but I imagine that I'll figure it out along the way.

As you grow up and get older I'm sure that I will adjust. I'm sure that little by little I will loosen my grip on the reins of your well-being that I currently hold so tightly. I'm not saying that I will ever stop worrying about you or trying to protect you, but I will trust in the Universe and in God's plan for you and know that you will always be protected.

Children are God's way of saving us.
They give us a second chance at getting it right.

Nancy Arroyo Ruffin

Part II:

FOR THE YOUNG LADIES

You more than anyone else deserve to be loved and to be happy.
Do not remain in any relationship that robs you of those two things.

Nancy Arroyo Ruffin

That's the way love goes

"Where do you think you're going?" Carlos snickered as he took a gulp out of his favorite mug. It was full to the brim with Budweiser and he always enjoyed drinking a nice cold one after a long work day. Dinner was ready and Isabella called out for Damarís and Carlitos (Carlos Jr.) to come eat as she finished getting ready for another night of dancing.

"Aye Carlos, you know Thursdays are Salsa nights down at the Copa," Isabella said. "And tonight El Gran Combo is going to be there directo de Puerto Rico."

"I haven't seen them play since the last time you knocked out that guy at Broadway 96. Remember that? Aye dios mio, I almost couldn't believe it. The only thing he did was offer me a drink after we danced."

"Damarís, Carlitos ven, dinner is served," she yelled. Damarís jumped off the top bunk bed and ran into the multi-purpose kitchen that also served as a dining room. The kitchen was small but still Isabella managed to fit a dinette and a washing machine in it. Carlitos followed behind his older sister and sat in his usual chair directly opposite from the old, white, now yellowish-brown Frigidaire refrigerator. The refrigerator was next to the stove and every time their mother fried food the grease from the frying pan ended up on the refrigerator.

The Yankees game was on TV and the only thing that Carlos loved more than a cold beer was The NY Yankees. If the Yankees were playing and losing the best thing to do was to disappear from his view. When the Yankees lost Carlos always took it so personally. He'd get angry, curse, call them bums and then unleash his madness on whoever was around him. Tonight they were losing 7-3 and if Isabella had plans to go dancing she'd better hope that the Yankees made a comeback.

Damarís and Carlitos sat at the kitchen table eating the arroz blanco, habichuelas and chuletas Isabella had cooked for dinner and listened to their mother tell her story. Damarís sat their silently but intrigued, knowing that it must have ended badly for whoever "the guy" was her mother was talking about. She knew her father was a traditional Puerto Rican man. He'd let his woman dance with other men because he too loved salsa and didn't see any harm in dancing. But a man offering to buy another man's woman a drink was a sign of disrespect, an unwritten rule, an imaginary line that you just didn't cross and if you did then you suffered the consequence.

Damarís didn't know if "the guy" from Broadway 96 knew that her mother was Carlos' woman but from the story Isabella was telling it didn't matter. He should have known. "Tonight, I'm going to dance all night just like that pink little Energizer bunny. Are you sure that you don't want to come?" Isabella asked Carlos excitedly while refilling his mug with another beer.

Her mother's tone reminded Damarís of the wishful tone in her and Carlitos' voices whenever they asked their father for something that they really wanted and knew they weren't going to get. As if saying it in this manner would somehow trick their father into thinking that he should get them whatever it was that they wanted. By Isabella's tone and the sparkle in her eye, Damarís knew her mother was hoping that their father would say yes. Isabella loved dancing and especially loved dancing with Carlos.

"I'm not going anywhere and neither are you," Carlos scowled. "Get in there and make sure the kids finished eating their dinner and get them ready for bed. They have school tomorrow."

Damarís and Carlitos sat in the small kitchen quiet as mice, motionless not wanting to bring any attention to them. Damarís knew this was coming. The Yankees lost and her father was not in a good mood.

"Pero amorcito, you said last week that I could go," Isabella whispered in a child-like tone that made her sound more like his daughter than his wife. As she began clearing the dinner dishes she said to Damarís, "Take Carlitos and get ready for bed," Damarís got up from the table and did as she was told because she knew this wasn't the time for a debate. If her father said it was time for bed then it was time for bed. Carlitos, however, was not as understanding.

"But ma, it's only 8 p.m. and our bedtime isn't until 10 o'clock." He said it so matter-of-factly as if this was a democracy and he really had a say.

"I don't care what time it is, go to bed now!" Isabella retorted. The kids walked quietly and quickly into the living room, scurrying through the sala, similar to the way cockroaches do when you turn on the light in a dark room. Damarís always found it funny to see them dash to the safety of the nearest crack or hole in the wall.

Carlos was still sitting in his favorite Lay-Z-boy chair in the living room. He refused to get rid of it even though it was falling apart. He originally purchased that chair for Isabella 13 years ago when she had given birth to Damarís. Throughout the years he slowly put his claim on it and now no one was allowed to sit on it. Not that anyone wanted to. It was torn and stained everywhere. The seat cushion was covered with an old black and red plaid pillow case that Isabella tore apart and then sewed back together. It smelled of old musk and tobacco. A combination of Carlos' old spice cologne and cigarette smoke was embedded in the fabric. It stuck out like a sore thumb. It was the only item that didn't match their newly purchased living room set.

The children gave their father a good night kiss on the cheek and although he was visibly upset he reciprocated and gave his children a kiss and a hug.

"I will come tuck you kids into bed in a few minutes," he said. That was the thing about Carlos, no matter how upset he was or how late he got home from work he always tucked his kids into bed.

Damarís and Carlitos went straight into their bedroom and closed the door. Damarís knew it was pointless. The door was not thick enough to block out the sounds of the next WWE match that was about to take place in the next room. Isabella and Carlos argued all the time and while Carlos didn't like hitting Isabella, sometimes he had to remind her that he was the *man* of the house. At least that's what he used to say after each of their matches. He would always tell Damarís, "Make sure you get a good education so that you can create your own life and not have to depend on a man for anything."

Whenever her parents fought, Damarís prayed that her mother would keep her mouth shut. If she remained quiet it would all be over fairly quickly. Her father just liked to feel powerful. He wanted to feel respected. After all, he was the man in the house.

War

It will come disguised

in silk and sweet tongue.

Fill your belly with myrrh

and tell you of all the ways

he will love thee.

Trace your body

like the Arabian peninsula

inhale your fragrance

like frankincense

sparse bunches of paired leaves

to make his home.

Entire cities

will be named

in your honor.

Flags resurrected

flown high

reminders of what

he has conquered.

Some call it love.

I call it war.

He ain't no wizard and this ain't Oz...

She always said he was her Fred Astaire. I've never seen Fred Astaire dance, but the way she talked about him he must have been a really good dancer. I loved watching them dance. When they danced it felt like the entire world stopped, opened up its mouth and sucked you in. Transporting you to a place far away from Brooklyn to a place where everything was colorful and bright; a place where good witches, fairies, ruby red slippers and yellow brick roads existed like in The Wizard of Oz.

Her feathered hair lightly swayed in the air as he would guide her with his hand into the next dance position. Gliding effortlessly on the dance floor he led and she pleasantly followed. The twists and turns were intricate yet whimsical. The type of dancing that could only be seen in a fairytale. Her body would flow easily and her dress would open up catching the wind underneath its wings like a bird in flight. When they danced it always felt like they were the only two in the room, but as soon as the music stopped so did the fairytale.

Skin

Ours was an unbridled love affair

Inverted vertebrae

against bare wall

tongue on skin

clenched teeth

your mouth in places

I never knew I had

your scent

familiar like the sound

of my own name.

I still wake

longing for your touch.

Skin open wound raw

because I was told

that's the only way to heal.

I couldn't tame you

you weren't meant for domestication.

Meant to roam free,

but I still remember

the first time you said "I love you"

a whisper barely audible

afraid of choking

on your words or mine

you preferred me voiceless

blank stare submissive

swallowing back years of lost time

waiting for you to change.

Sudoku

Loving him

was an unsolvable

Sudoku puzzle

a bunch of numbers in squares

that just didn't fit.

Salvation

won't come through prayer,
even though I've tried
to free myself
from the temptation
of his kiss,
his touch,
the way he whispers my name
when we make love.

His hands
paint hieroglyphics on my skin.
paleolithic carvings
buried in the bowels
of past mistakes.
He is my salvation
and I carry traces
of his love
like a lost soul
trying to find its way home.

Rum Soaked Rainbows

I want to write my secrets

on your skin

with blood tears

so that you never

question my love

even on the days

when I tell you I don't.

Learn me

when you can't

figure me out.

Taste me,

even when

your palette

wants to regurgitate me

like last night's spoiled milk.

Know that the future

exists between my thighs.

Generations waiting

with dried sweat on curved brow

heart spinning blues and stuffed shadows

 drunk off rum soaked rainbows.

For the men who love us

He wore love on his arm

a reminder of all he had given her

he loved her dutifully

in the morning

in the evening

and until the sun rose again

her warmth had become his security

seeking her out whenever he was afraid

she was the sun at dusk that kissed the horizon goodnight

and he, he was the sky that patiently waited.

Baby girl you're a star.

Don't let them tell you you're not.

J. Cole

Re-Birth

I will teach you how to give birth

shed misconceptions like reptilian skin

peel back layers 'til you

see more than just pigment.

Reborn

African queen

like Kahina, Amina, and Cleopatra.

Who led you to believe that you are not beautiful?

As if to be black

is a curse inflicted by the Gods.

You are life's energy

like the softness of water

the guiding light of the moon

the ebony richness of soil

and the deep silence of night.

You are Yin.

Let all who cross your path

bow their heads in respect

for you are crowned empress.

Old world customs

and new age religion

will make you question

your existence

but when they ask

stand tall

spine erect

and tell them

you were born

to carry entire nations

on your back.

Part III:

FOR THE ELDERS

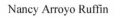

It is often nature's way that we often feel closer to distant generations than to the generation immediately preceding us.

Igor Stravinsky

Doña Paula

WHEN I WAS YOUNGER I SPENT A lot of time at my grandmother's house. She lived down the block and around the corner from the apartment I grew up in (in fact, she still lives there). She is as much a part of the neighborhood as the foundation that her building is built on. Everyone knows Doña Paula, the petite little old woman who stands just under 5 ft. tall and weighs about 80lbs soak and wet.

Her long locks once the color of night have been cropped into an unruly short cut now covered in shimmering silver strands of gray. At 88 years old she has lived a full life that at times has been rewarding and at other times heartbreaking.

She raised her children as a single mother and has also been integral in raising her grandchildren. She has survived domestic abuse, has lived through the murder of one of her sons, has mourned the death of a grandson, and has had to bear witness to the perils that addiction and substance abuse has had on her family.

She migrated to New York from Puerto Rico in the mid 50's and despite living here most of her life has never learned to speak English. My grandfather, an alcoholic and heavy cigarette smoker, died of lung cancer leaving her a widow to raise her children in a city where everything was alien to her.

Making a life for herself and her children in a new environment wasn't easy, but women are strong and resilient if nothing else. Being married to an abusive drunk who often said, "¿Pa' que bañarme? Sólo las personas que huelen se bañan." *"Why bathe? only people who smell take baths"*, only strengthened her resolve and determination to make a better life for her family.

My mother often shares fond memories of my grandfather. She talks about how much she loved him, but always prefaces her statements with "he was so good when he wasn't drunk." I understand the love a daughter has for her father, but when I think of my grandfather all I envision is him beating on my grandmother's petite frame.

He would put her out into the hallway of their building like last night's trash and lock her out of their apartment leaving her to sleep at the foot of the door like an animal; promising that he would do the same to my mother and her siblings if any of them tried to open the door to let their mother in.

The stories I've heard about him are disturbing. Like the time my mother told me a story about how excited she was to go to a party and after getting dressed and all prettied up he ordered her to get undressed during one of his alcohol induced rants. He refused to let her go even though he initially gave her permission to attend. He was cruel and mean, heartless even.

I find it hard to believe that I could have loved a man like him especially knowing how much I love my grandmother. Her body bent with age still gives the most soul filling hugs. Her glistening cataract filled eyes still light up every time she sees one of her grandchildren or great grandchildren and her small tender hands still make the best cup of coffee I have ever tasted. As small as she may be she is the glue that holds our family together and thinking about someone mistreating her stirs something up inside me like a volcano that is ready to erupt.

My grandmother is very protective of her family. There were many nights I would awaken from my sleep to find her getting dressed.

"¿Pa' donde vas abuela?" I'd ask. "Voy a ver si veo a las muchachas por allí," she'd reply.

She'd go patrolling the Brooklyn streets at all hours of the night searching for my aunts because it was 3 in the morning and they weren't home yet.

They were young adults infatuated with the NY club scene and they went clubbing all the time. My traditional Puerto Rican grandmother did not understand this new wave independence or why her daughters loved being out so much. Her philosophy was that decent girls did not stay out all night. Not wanting her to go out in the middle of the night alone I'd get up and roam the streets with her. I couldn't have been more than 7 or 8 years old and although I couldn't protect her I at least found solace in knowing that she wasn't walking the streets by herself.

A couple of months ago while at work, I received a call from my aunt. I missed the call, but the voicemail message said,

"Nancy, I'm on my way to the hospital with mom. Call me." After taking my grandmother to what was supposed to be a routine medical check-up, the doctor discovered that her heart was not beating how it was supposed to. Her pulse, which should have been at 60 beats per minute, was beating at 40 beats per minute and he was concerned.

He immediately made the decision to have her admitted and she was taken by ambulance to Beth Israel Medical Center. After a number of routine tests and an EKG were performed, it was determined that to get her heart beating regularly my grandmother would require a pacemaker.

She is the heart of my family and although logically I know there will come a time when she will no longer physically be here the reality of that hit home when I saw her in that hospital bed helpless and scared. It was like watching a child in the hospital for the first time. She was confused and afraid. Not being able to speak English or understand what the doctors were saying to her only added to the stress and fear she was feeling. She was now completely dependent on her family to get her through one of the most frightful experiences she has ever encountered.

The after effects of the anesthesia had my grandmother a bit disoriented. Her behavior was similar to that of a person suffering from dementia. She wasn't aware of her surroundings. She kept thinking she was home. She was argumentative and combative with the hospital staff. She kept trying to pull the bandages off her chest where the incision was made to install the pacemaker and no matter how many times we tried to explain to her where she was, she couldn't comprehend.

It was heartbreaking seeing her in such a helpless state. This strong woman who has survived so much in her life, who has never depended on anyone for anything, was now depending on everyone else to take care of her and is now dependent on a machine to keep her heart beating. Life has a funny way of kicking us in our rear ends and making us stop and re-evaluate our lives and our relationships.

For my grandmother, it was making her realize that at 88 years old it was time for her to stop taking care of everybody else. It was time for her family to now take care of her. Sometimes we take people for granted and sometimes it isn't until something extreme happens that we realize something has to change. The two days my grandmother spent in the hospital were a wakeup call that the time had come for the people that she has devoted her life caring for, needed to start taking care of her.

We have to take care of our elders. We have to appreciate them. We have to protect them. It is time for us to repay them for all they have done for us. Don't wait until it's too late to show someone how much they are loved and appreciated. For me, that event forced me to think about my relationship with my grandmother. Have I done enough to take care of her? Have I showed her how much I appreciate her? Have I been a good granddaughter? Have I made her proud?

My grandmother's hands

have massaged tired limbs and weary hearts.

They have cleaned homes,

swept floors,

toiled grass roots in cemented lands,

laid bricks and mortar

for future generations.

My grandmother's hands

have coddled bodega lotto dreams

like her new born child.

They are lamb's wool on naked skin.

My grandmother's hands

have clasped arctic tenement building floors

shielding 5 finger back slaps

that burned souls like hot coals.

Pink-grey cinders of ash

marked with years of resentment

for the lives they couldn't save.

My grandmother's hands

have molded boys into men,

girls into women with strength

like old family traditions.

Overflowing with unfulfilled promises

that time has carried away,

and all that is left are the years

of struggle permanently engraved

on the palms of

my grandmother's hands.

La grifa

Me llaman la grifa

niña linda

pelo malo

because

it wouldn't obey

untamable beast

told to relax

as the lie (lye) concoction

burned the kink out of my hair

erasing temporarily the part

of me that I hated the most.

Genetically made up to be wild

not to be tamed

or managed

or straightened

or subdued

or laid flatly with

no body or bounce

No...that

could never be me.

For ...

I am too relentless

to conform

to transform

to be altered

into something

that I wasn't really destined

to be.

History, despite its wrenching pain, cannot be unlived, but if faced with courage, need not be lived again.

Maya Angelou

History

She is a living record

of what can't be found in history books

for they can never capture

the layers of life

that she wears on her face like armor.

Each wrinkle a reminder of a past victory.

No nip and tuck to help erase

the bitter winters of loneliness.

No sweet lullaby to sing

for the aspirations she carried on her back.

Her eyes,

heavy from centuries of disappointment

have witnessed

birth,

death,

love,

hate.

Her lips, have only spoken the truth

even when she wasn't understood.

Navigating through unfamiliar places,

with strange faces,

and labeled an alien.

A word used to describe

anything that is different.

Never fulfilling prophecies
of men destined to be kings, but instead
nurtured boys whose lives would end
before they began
like Emmett Till,
Ramarley Graham,
Sean Bell,
Trayvon Martin,
or the ones who never make the news
like Manual Diaz or Cesar Cruz.

Searching for justice
in a foreign land,
ambition is now placed
in the hands of future generations
who don't even know
the strength they possess.
Honor, power, self-respect
once petroglyphs etched on stone
are now an apparition
that have been replaced
by half-naked young women
diminishing their self-worth

to chase a net worth

provided by media empires

designed to distract us.

Little girl,

you are beauty,

you are love,

you are special.

Little boy,

you are strength,

you are honor,

you are greatness.

Reclaim what is rightfully yours.

For the footsteps of our ancestors

have long faded

and history has pushed its way

into the present.

We, are here now.

We, are history

that hasn't been

written yet.

Roots

I carry history in my hair.

Generations of thick tangled tresses

colored with shame at the roots.

Stripped, dyed, burned, fried

trying unsuccessfully to alter its DNA.

Since birth, my hair has danced violently

to a beat of its own.

Tautly twined coils

stretched like the goatskin

that cover djembe drums

each lock relentlessly rebelling.

Defiant like sugar cane

trying to make its way through concrete.

Often curled in bouncing question marks

unsure of its own beauty.

For generations these strands

have carried inherited misconceptions

that I will pass down to my daughter

as they were passed down to me.

Recycling inferiority complexes

neatly packaged on assembly lines

and carefully placed on the top shelves

of our pharmacies and for $7.99 you too

can have soft, beautiful, manageable hair.

What I learned from my grandfather

can be summarized

in three words:

Que se muera.

Orgullo (Pride)

WHEN I WAS A YOUNG GIRL I spent every Sunday at my grandfather's house in Bedford-Stuyvesant, Brooklyn. My family and I went there every week, religiously like it was church. My parents, sister, aunts, uncles, and cousins made their way to the 3 bedroom apartment that my father and his siblings grew up in to have Sunday dinner. While dinner was what brought us all together, it was not the reason everyone visited my grandfather each Sunday. It was about family. It was about spending time with each other, it was about catching up on the week's events, but it was also about nurturing the family ties left to us by our ancestors.

It was where the adults would plan our annual summer vacations to Las Villas in upstate Platekill, NY. It was where promises were made like when my mother vowed to my grandfather to never cut my sister's dark wavy locks because long beautiful hair was revered in our family. It was where my then 7 yr. old sister got her first lesson in female anatomy when she blurted out at the dinner table, "Mommy? What's a vagina?" when my cousin and I in our mischievous behavior refused to tell her the meaning of the new word I'd just learned. I got in trouble for that.

It was where we'd get chastised by our Titi Cherry for spinning ourselves on the swivel styled leather dining room seats. It's funny what you remember as a kid. Being part of a large Puerto Rican family instilled in me a strong love for familia, cultura, and orgullo. I was taught to be proud of who I was and where I came from. They are the same lessons that I will pass on to the young people in my life.

However, understanding who I truly was and where I came from was not something that I knew then. As a child I wasn't taught much about Puerto Rican history. For me, cultura were the sleepless nights spent in my grandfather's house watching the grown-ups guayando platanos to make pasteles for the Thanksgiving and Christmas holidays. It was watching the adults become transfixed to the television whenever Walter Mercado came on and revealed to them their fate through their horoscopes.

Orgullo was me proudly wearing the brown leather chancletas with Puerto Rico inscribed on them in bright golden letters. It was being able to boast to my friends that I'd spent my summer vacation on la Isla del Encanto visiting my aunt and cousins, and familia didn't necessarily always mean someone in your bloodline, but instead could be found in that one friend who you proudly said was your cousin even though there was no ancestral relation.

Growing up and attending school in New York City I wasn't taught about the little island in the Caribbean where my ancestors came from. I didn't know that we officially became a U. S. territory in 1917 after President Woodrow Wilson passed the Jones Act. I was not taught about Pura Belpre and how she was the first Latina librarian in New York City or about how Pedro Albizu Campos was used as a human guinea pig and was the subject of human radiation experiments while in a United States prison; or how I didn't know that he was also the nephew of Juan Morel Campos, one of Puerto Rico's most distinguished composers. I learned about him later on in life despite attending a junior high school that was named after him because they didn't teach me about him there either.

There's a long list of Puerto Ricans who have contributed to politics, music, and the arts. We have produced poets (Julia de Burgos), astronauts (Joseph Michael Acaba), scientists (Olga D. Gonzalez-Sanabria), even Supreme Court justices (Sonia Sotomayor). We are more than just Marc Anthony and Jennifer Lopez, although their contribution to the arts and music should be commended.

I spent most of my childhood being a proud Puerto Rican, but really had no clue as to what exactly I was proud of. For a long time when someone asked me "What do Puerto Ricans have to be proud of?" I could never give a well thought out and educated answer. To me, pride had always been about love for the culture, food, music, and familia even though we have many other reasons to be proud. We are after all more than just salsa music, good food, and an annual parade down Fifth Avenue. We come from a long line of hardworking individuals, many who have made indelible contributions to the world we live in, be it on the island or here in the

States. It wasn't until I was older and started educating myself that I learned exactly what I should be proud of.

Now that I am a mother it is my responsibility to educate my daughter and the other young people in my life on their history. Puerto Rican history is not taught in American schools and the education our children are getting today is mediocre at best. So if our school systems are not teaching us our history or are teaching it inaccurately, who will? Whose responsibility does it become to teach us about ourselves, about our accomplishments, about our greatness?

Ensuring that our children develop a strong sense of worth is part of our jobs as parents. In order for us to truly love ourselves and see our value and what we bring to this world starts from understanding who we are as a people.

D o not be afraid to color outside the lines or to make mistakes. Take risks and do not be afraid to fail. Know that when the world knocks you down, the best revenge is to get up and continue forging ahead. Do not be afraid to be different or to stand up for what's right. Never quiet your voice to make someone else feel comfortable. No one remembers the person that fits in. It's the one who stands out that people will not be able to forget. - Nancy Arroyo Ruffin

Mamí always said

there's nothing

some music

and a home cooked meal

can't fix.

Pa' Celia

WHEN I FIRST SAW CELIA PERFORM years ago at a concert in D.C. I did not realize that I was witnessing a legend. Her bigger than life persona left an indelible impact on me that I did not realize until I became an adult. She was the consummate performer. A woman who loved what she did and her fans loved her even more. She was beautiful, proud, talented, and she was Latina. She forever will be La Reina de la Salsa. La Negra que tiene tumbao who reminded us que La Vida es un Carnaval. Ella es el ritmo que une a la gente. She gave me my life's anthem and for that I am grateful.

"Todo aquel que piense que la vida es desigual,
tiene que saber que no es asi,
que la vida es una hermosura, hay que vivirla.
Todo aquel que piense que esta solo y que esta mal,
tiene que saber que no es asi,
que en la vida no hay nadie solo, siempre hay alguien.

Ay, no hay que llorar, que la vida es un carnaval,
es mas bello vivir cantando."

– La Vida es un Carnaval lyrics, Celia Cruz

To the beat of the drum

I was born to the beat of the drum

in the wilds of Nigeria

where my lineage began

to Yoruba swaying hips.

Warrior woman

like Anacaona or Yuisa

Taino cacique

descendent of Queens

though many would have me

believe otherwise.

As if I can ever deny

the ran kan kan rhythm

of Tito or the sweet azúcar of Celia

that runs through my veins

life inducing spirituals

sung in foreign tongues

on ghetto street corners

celebrating La Fiesta de Pilito

con El Gran Combo, Hector, y La Lupe

en la casa de don Daniél.

We dance to the beat of this drum

on the streets of Humacao

to the streets of El Barrio,

Brooklyn, y el Bronx.

Old men slap fichas on

makeshift tables

shouting Capicu

and eating bacalaitos

from the corner cuchifrito.

We make love to the

beat of the drum

so we can feel

the vibrations of our souls

the most beautiful music

we will ever make.

Un verano en Nueva York

blasted from Blanco's night club,

kids on front stoops

mothers with baby strollers

women parading

up and down the block

tight jeans,

tight blouses,

4-inch high heels.

Faces fully made up

but nowhere to go.

No matter how dreary and gray our homes are, we people of flesh and blood would rather live there than in any other country, be it ever so beautiful. There is no place like home.

L. Frank Baum, *The Wizard of Oz*

No place like home

When you grow up in the hood you immediately become identified by the block that you live on. You somehow become a living, breathing representation of that street. I grew up on South 10th street and Bedford Avenue in a modest sized 5 story apartment building that was located between the local bodega owned by Fidel and a tire shop owned by our neighbor Joey.

The building was painted a dull lifeless gray and the hallways were always dark and gloomy except for the one light that flickered on and off at the end of the hallway were the staircase was located. To the right of the stairs was a door that led into the backyard of the building. The backyard was akin to a junkyard. Tenants would throw dirty diapers back there, half-eaten food, old clothes, shoes, and anything else they were too lazy to dispose of properly. Bags of garbage would be kept there awaiting pick up from the sanitation trucks. There were many times I'd look out my bedroom window, which overlooked the backyard, and see huge rats digging through the garbage for food. I like to believe those experiences were preparing me for life in the real world. Anybody can be book smart, but not everybody is born with the gritty survival skills necessary to deal with the curve balls life often throws at us.

It was normal to see the older neighborhood men congregating on the block in front of Fidel's store or see them sitting on milk crates playing dominoes yelling capicu. It didn't matter the time of day, people were always outside; old people, young people, children, infants, everyone. The younger adults would often hang out in front of their building and sit on the stoop. You'd see mothers who should have been home with their children hanging out in the park with their baby strollers while their babies slept. For some reason people felt like they were missing something if they weren't outside.

Unlike the New Jersey suburb I currently live in, there weren't any after school sports programs or dance classes. The only extracurricular activities for kids included going to the rundown playgrounds that were often shared with the neighborhood crackheads or hanging out on the street corner. Both of which made it very easy to get caught up in things that you probably shouldn't be doing.

Yet, there was no place like NYC. In the summertime the boys played wiffle ball while the girls played hopscotch. On the occasions where the temperature hit the 90 degree mark someone would bring out the wrench and open the pump. The water would blast out of the cast iron devices like a roaring river cooling off overheated hands, heads, and hearts of the young and old alike. Bathing in it like we were home and letting the coolness of the water wash away all of the days grittiness. There weren't country clubs or summer trips to the shore but this was home and there's no place like home.

De donde vengo yo (Where I'm from)

This want of knowing

is greater than the need

of oxygen in my lungs

because to be alive

and not know who you are

or where you're from

is not the same as living.

De donde vengo yo is not a question.

It is a statement.

An affirmation of where I'm from.

It's my grandmother's hands

that have dried crying eyes

and mended broken hearts.

It's my mother's strength

that she wears everyday

like her rosario.

Where I'm from,

the cool breeze

knows nothing

of cruel winters.

It's where the rain makes love

to the earth every night

and her harvest

can nourish

an entire village.

It's where the sun lays its lips

on her sugar cane skin,

promising to always keep her warm.

It's where the moonlight dances

to the timeless rhythms of the drums.

De donde vengo yo

pride is heard

in the song of the coqui.

It's where love

is felt in the sound

of her bendicion.

It's where a tasa de café

is a sacred experience

to be shared

with the one you love

over the early morning sunrise.

De donde vengo yo

the 1950's migration

was the promise of new life.

But weary limbs

and losing lotto numbers

were reminders that

in this country

you need more than
$1 and a dream.

Where I'm from
I was taught to invest in me
because de donde vengo yo
is where Supreme Court Justices are born.
Where I'm from
you do not need a dictionary
to communicate with your people
porque allí se habla Español
all the time.

De donde vengo yo
is seen every second Sunday in June
taking over Fifth Avenue.
De donde vengo yo
las navidades son parrandas,
los 3 reyes magos, y un lechon.
It is where, si no hay para todo
no hay para nadie.

De donde vengo yo is not a question.
It is a statement.
An affirmation of where I'm from.
A testament to those
who came before me.

Underneath my bed

is a treasure chest

spilling old pictures

a sift of lost faces

to remind me

that I am from those moments

snapped before I existed.

De allí es de donde vengo yo.

The first step - especially for young people with energy and drive and talent, - to controlling your world, is to control your culture. To model and demonstrate the kind of world you demand to live in. To write the books. Make the music. Shoot the films. Paint the art.

Chuck Palahniuk

ALSO BY NANCY ARROYO RUFFIN

Available for purchase on amazon.com and barnesandnoble.com

www.nancyruffin.net

Made in the USA
Coppell, TX
04 October 2020